PIANO | VOCAL | GUITAR ■ CD   **VOLUME 82**

PIANO PLAY-ALONG

LIONEL RICHIE

Cover photo © Alan Silfen

ISBN 978-1-4234-3431-3

HAL•LEONARD®
CORPORATION
7777 W. BLUEMOUND RD. P.O. BOX 13819 MILWAUKEE, WI 53213

Visit Hal Leonard Online at
www.halleonard.com

CONTENTS

ALL NIGHT LONG
(All Night)

Words and Music by
LIONEL RICHIE

Moderate Caribbean feel

Da da

Oh

Well, my friends, the time has come.
Peo-ple danc-ing all in the street,

Raise the roof and
see the rhy-thm all

9

long. _____

Ev - 'ry - one _____ you meet, _____ they're

jam - min' in _____ the street, _____ all night long. _____

SAY YOU, SAY ME

from the Motion Picture WHITE NIGHTS

Words and Music by
LIONEL RICHIE

lieve in who ___ you are; ___ you are a shin - ing star. ___

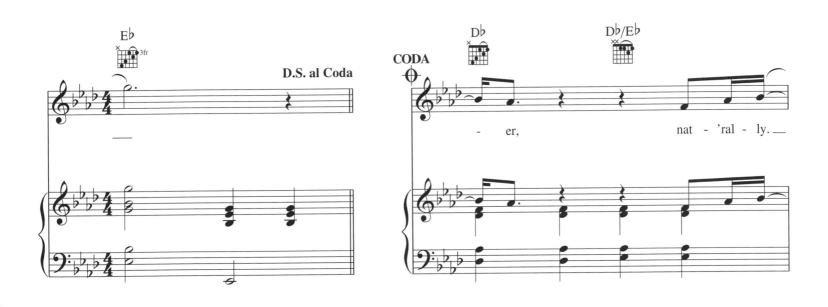

D.S. al Coda

CODA

- er, nat - 'ral - ly. ___

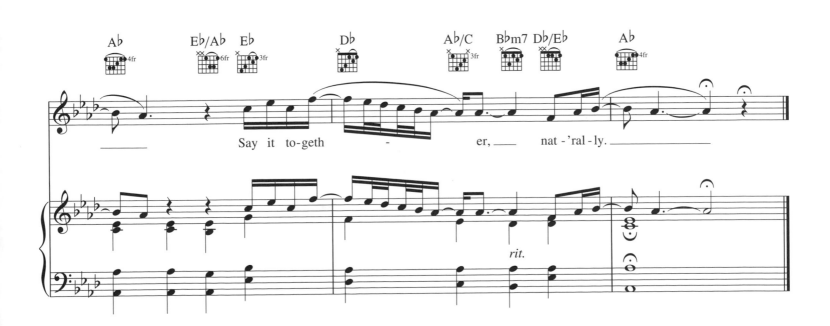

Say it to-geth - er, ___ nat -'ral - ly. ___

rit.

LADY

Words and Music by
LIONEL RICHIE

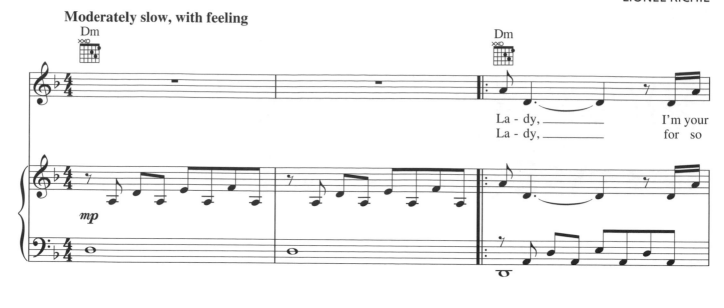

PENNY LOVER

Words and Music by LIONEL RICHIE
and BRENDA HARVEY-RICHIE

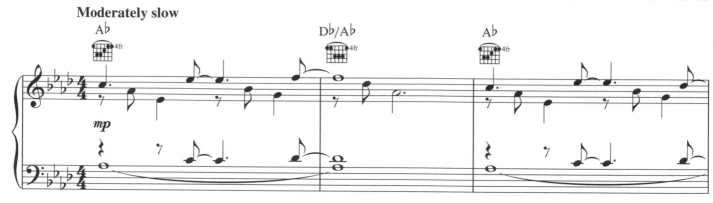

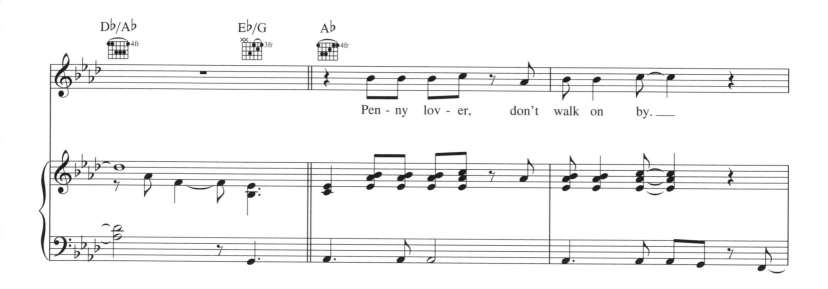

Pen - ny lov - er, don't walk on by. ___

Pen - ny lov - er, don't you make me cry. ___   Can't you see, girl, who my

you came a - long ___ and cap - tured my heart. ___

Now my love is some - where lost ___ in your ___ kiss. When I'm

all a - lone ___ it's you that I miss. Girl, a love like yours is hard ___ to re -

sist. Oh. ___

’cause when a man’s ___ in love ___ he’s on - ly got one sto -

- ry.

That’s why my love is some-where lost ___ in your ___

___ kiss. When I’m lost and a - lone ___ it’s you

that I miss. With a love like yours, it’s hard to re - sist. Oh, ___ oh. _

make me cry. _____ (Oh, _____ Pen - ny ba - by.) _____ Pen - ny lov - er, don't you

walk on by. _____ (Don't you walk _ on by.) _____

(Spoken:) I remember the first time I saw you, baby. Pen - ny lov - er, don't you

make me cry. _____ *You had that look in your eye, you had that*

STILL

Words and Music by
LIONEL RICHIE

Cmaj7　　　　　　　　　　C9　　C7　　Bb/A　　C7/G

go, _____ where'd we go? _____
me. _____ 'Cause I need - ed you so _____

Fmaj7　　　　　　　Dm7　　　　G

Lost what we both had found, _____ you know __ we
_____ des - p'rate - ly. We were __ too

Cmaj7　　　　　　　　C9　　C7　　Bb/A　　C7/G

let _____ each oth - er down, ⎫ but then,
blind _____ to see. ⎭

Fmaj7　　　　　　　Am7/E　　Dm7

most of all, _____ I do love _____ you _____

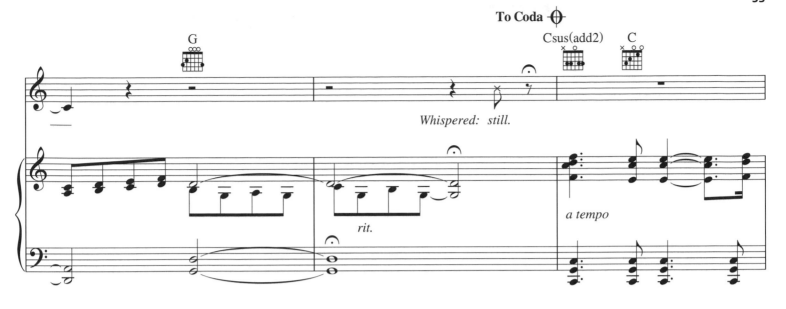

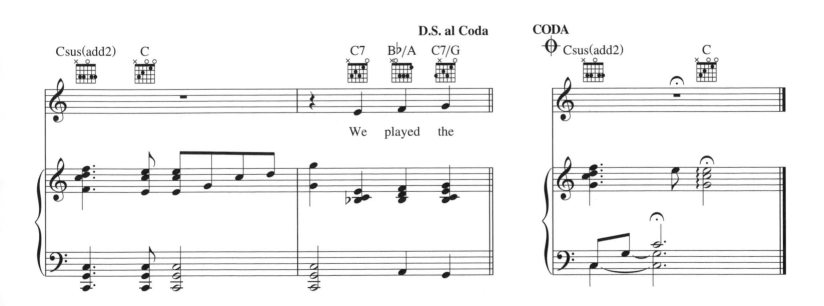

THREE TIMES A LADY

Words and Music by
LIONEL RICHIE

Thanks for the

times that you've giv - en me. ___ The

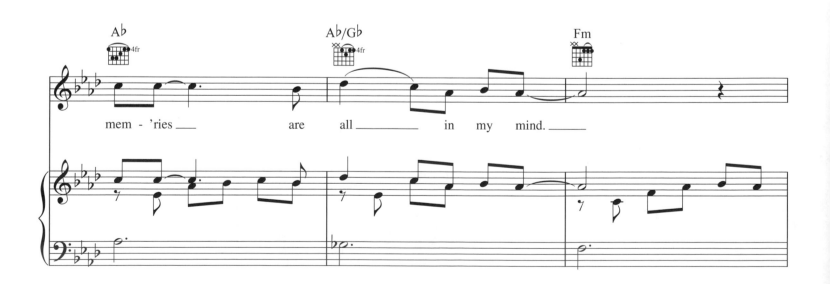

mem - 'ries ___ are all ___ in my mind. ___

and I love _____ you. _____ Yes, you're once, __

twice, __ three times a la - dy,

and I love _____ you, _____

I love _____ you. _____

part. _____

Ooh, _____ ooh, _____

ooh, _____ ooh, _____ ooh. _____

39

TRULY

Words and Music by
LIONEL RICHIE

1
Dm7
F/G
G
Gsus
G
al - ways be there.
2
Dm7
F/G
G
Gsus
G
love will last for - ev - er. Be - cause I'm
C(add9)
C7
Fmaj7
8fr
tru - ly, tru - ly in love with you, girl.
F/G
C(add9)
C7
I'm tru - ly, head o - ver

STUCK ON YOU

Words and Music by
LIONEL RICHIE

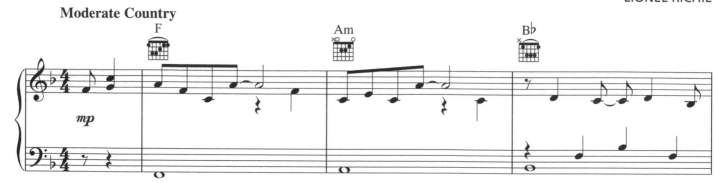

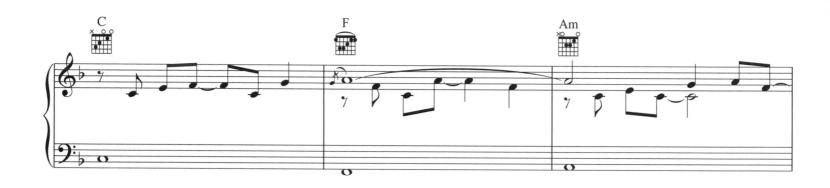

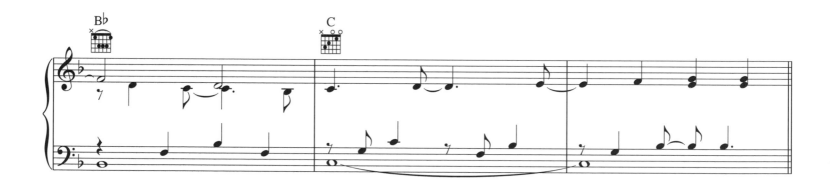

(1.,3.) Stuck on you, ___ I've got this feel - in' down deep in my soul ___

(2.) Stuck on you, ___ been a fool too ___ long, I guess it's

might-y glad you stayed. _
might-y glad you stayed. _

Oh, I'm leav - ing on ____ that mid - night train to - mor -